Wisdom
for
Dads

ZondervanPublishingHouse
Grand Rapids, Michigan

A Division of HarperCollins*Publishers*

Wisdom For Dads
© 1996 by The Zondervan Corporation

ISBN: 0-310-96732-5

Requests for information should be addressed to:
 ♣ ZondervanPublishingHouse
  Grand Rapids, Michigan 49530

Printed in the United States of America

96 97 98 / RRD-H / 3 2 1

Table of Contents

Introduction

Being a dad in the '90s is a great challenge. There are increasing demands on your time and energy with each new day. You're expected to be the 'expert' in so many areas and to a variety of people—your mate, your children, your boss or employees, friends, neighbors.

Featuring quotes from a diverse group of popular contemporary authors combined with Scripture passages from the New International Version text, *Wisdom For Dads* offers a unique source of encouragement and direction for today's busy man. Short quotes from well-known authors such as Chuck Swindoll, Dr. Larry Crabb, Bill Hybels, D. James Kennedy, Ken Gire and many more provide insight and advice on marriage, being a godly man, being a friend, an example in the workplace, a spiritual leader, a neighbor, and, of course, being a father.

Wisdom For . . . Your Role As Husband

Husbands, love your wives, just as Christ loved the church and gave himself up for her to make her holy, cleansing her by the washing with water through the word, and to present her to himself as a radiant church, without stain or wrinkle or any other blemish, but holy and blameless. — EPHESIANS 5:25–27

✒

Marriage has taught me that I am neither all-sufficient nor totally self-sufficient. I *need* a wife. I need her support, her insight, her discernment, her counsel, her love, her presence, and her efficiency. She is not my crutch . . . but she is my God-given companion and partner, ever aware of my moods and my needs. She hears my secrets and keeps them well. She knows my faults and forgives them often. She feels my failures and apprehensions and encourages me through them. — CHARLES R. SWINDOLL, *GROWING STRONG IN THE SEASONS OF LIFE*

The LORD God said, "It is not good for the man to be alone. I will make a helper suitable for him." —GENESIS 2:18

☙

By wisdom a house is built, and through understanding it is established; through knowledge its rooms are filled with rare and beautiful treasures. —PROVERBS 24:3–4

☙

A good relationship is one in which *each member willingly and actively devotes whatever he or she has to give to the well-being of the other.* In such a relationship, the highest criterion for deciding what to do at any moment is a person's understanding before God of what would be the greatest service he or she can offer to the other. —DR. LARRY CRABB, *MEN & WOMEN: ENJOYING THE DIFFERENCE*

☙

Love is patient, love is kind. It does not envy, it does not boast, it is not proud. It is not rude, it is not self-seeking, it is not easily angered, it keeps no record of wrongs. Love does not delight in evil but rejoices with the truth. It always protects, always trusts, always hopes, always perseveres. Love never fails. —1 CORINTHIANS 13:4–8a

☙

Each one of you ... must love his wife as he loves himself, and the wife must respect her husband. —EPHESIANS 5:33

❧

Husband . . . you need to take an honest, realistic look at your wife. You also need to hear what she's saying. And why she is saying it. You would do well to imagine yourself in her place for a change. . . . Visualize yourself trying to find meaning and purpose in the limited space her responsibilities require of her. Imagine trying to respond to *your* expectations and demands. —CHARLES R. SWINDOLL, *STRESS FRACTURES*

❧

A husband's authority to *wisely serve* his wife with the *resources of his masculinity* requires that he involve himself deeply in the affairs of his family and that he serve them as advocate. It requires that he provide them with love and direction in accordance with his understanding of God's character and their needs. —DR. LARRY CRABB, *MEN & WOMEN: ENJOYING THE DIFFERENCE*

❧

The husband is the head of the wife as Christ is the head of the church, his body, of which he is the Savior. Now as the church submits to Christ, so also wives should submit to their husbands in everything. —EPHESIANS 5:23–24

❧

It is misleading to define *headship* as a husband's right to decide something for his wife and then to require her submissive cooperation with his decision. Defining headship centrally as decision-making authority puts the wife in a position of subordination to a despotic authority. It creates a kind of hierarchical arrangement that blocks the growth of intimacy. Order is achieved at the expense of passion. —DR. LARRY CRABB, *MEN & WOMEN: ENJOYING THE DIFFERENCE*

❧

You want a wife who is gracious, forgiving, tolerant, and supportive? Start with her husband! It will roll from your soul to hers, my friend. As our Savior puts it, "Treat her exactly as you would like her to treat you." —CHARLES R. SWINDOLL, *GROWING STRONG IN THE SEASONS OF LIFE*

❧

Do to others as you would have them do to you. —LUKE 6:31

❧

Husbands, love your wives and do not be harsh with them. —COLOSSIANS 3:19

❧

When a man understands a woman, he is more likely to exercise his authority to serve, not by making occasional decisions or exhibiting his strength, but by being the advocate she desires and by moving tenderly toward

her with a smile in his eyes that tells her she is enjoyed.
—DR. LARRY CRABB, *MEN & WOMEN: ENJOYING THE DIFFERENCE*

⋘⋙

Have you a fragile butterfly who needs reassurance,
room to become? . . . Are you generous enough to put
away the net and let others enjoy her too? She's the
Lord's you know . . . not *your* possession. . . . If you
release her to spread her lovely wings for His glory, she
won't fly away forgetting and forsaking her roots. She will
flutter and flourish, adding dimensions of delight you
would never otherwise know. — CHARLES R. SWINDOLL,
GROWING STRONG IN THE SEASONS OF LIFE

⋘⋙

"This is now bone of my bones and flesh of my flesh;
she shall be called 'woman,' for she was taken out of
man."

For this reason a man will leave his father and mother and be united to his wife, and they will become one
flesh. — GENESIS 2:23–24

⋘⋙

Marriage should be honored by all, and the marriage
bed kept pure, for God will judge the adulterer and all the
sexually immoral. — HEBREWS 13:4

❧

The husband should fulfill his marital duty to his wife, and likewise the wife to her husband. The wife's body does not belong to her alone but also to her husband. In the same way, the husband's body does not belong to him alone but also to his wife. — 1 Corinthians 7:3–4

❧

Husbands ought to love their wives as their own bodies. He who loves his wife loves himself. After all, no one ever hated his own body, but he feeds and cares for it, just as Christ does the church—for we are members of his body. —Ephesians 5:28–30

❧

Directions to the husband specifically include nourishing his wife (providing for her needs) and cherishing (tenderly handling) her according to a thought-through understanding of her sensitivities (Ephesians 5:29; 1 Peter 3:7), whether it is in the tender, intimate life-generating physical relationship or in the confidence with which he approaches decisions in life. — Dr. Larry Crabb, Men & Women: Enjoying The Difference

❧

Husbands, in the same way be considerate as you live with your wives, and treat them with respect as the weaker partner and as heirs with you of the gracious gift of life, so that nothing will hinder your prayers. — 1 Peter 3:7

❧

Just as God calls people to work he has already enabled them to do, so he has designed men and women to relate in unique ways, and with his good plan in mind, he releases them to gladly accept their divinely appointed assignments. —DR. LARRY CRABB, *MEN & WOMEN: ENJOYING THE DIFFERENCE*

❧

What is an authentic marriage? It's a marriage where differences are seen as blessings. Where spouses really feel loved. And where routine gives way to conversation, fun, and romance. —BILL HYBELS, *HONEST TO GOD?*

❧

May your fountain be blessed, and may you rejoice in the wife of your youth. —PROVERBS 5:18

❧

When a man's purposes are godly, that is, when he is ambitious for God's glory and concerned with other-centered relating, he will experience a stability that anchors him through emotional ups and downs ... and a noble desire for tender, caring, intimate involvement with people, primarily his wife. —DR. LARRY CRABB, *MEN & WOMEN: ENJOYING THE DIFFERENCE*

❧❧

Every married woman longs to be loved by a truly masculine man—not an emasculated man devoid of energy, spirit, and confidence, or a macho cowboy who uses cheap bravado to prop up his male insecurities, but a God-honoring man who is secure enough to be divinely elastic. This brand of man can be both strong and sensitive. Such men free women to respond with respect and love. —BILL HYBELS, *HONEST TO GOD?*

❧❧

Husbands and wives should . . . communicate openly and honestly. . . . where each person works hard to understand both the other's point of view and whatever deeper concerns may lie beneath the disagreement. Sincere efforts to listen in an atmosphere of mutual submission may lead to a happy resolution satisfying to both parties. — DR. LARRY CRABB, *MEN & WOMEN: ENJOYING THE DIFFERENCE*

❧❧

Attempts to build a marriage by following rules or conforming to roles never quite produces a fluid, dynamic, natural union of two people becoming one. Something deeper is present in a good marriage. —DR. LARRY CRABB, *MEN & WOMEN: ENJOYING THE DIFFERENCE*

✍

To the married I give this command (not I, but the Lord): A wife must not separate from her husband. . . . And a husband must not divorce his wife. —1 CORINTHIANS 7:10–11

✍

Hatred stirs up dissension, but love covers over all wrongs. —PROVERBS 10:12

✍

Married folks would do well to think *less* about doing what good husbands and wives should do or whether they are properly taking their humanness into account, and *more* about how self-directed so much of their activity really is. Rather than figuring out practical ways to improve our marriages, perhaps we need to realize how badly and how often we need forgiveness. —DR. LARRY CRABB, *MEN & WOMEN: ENJOYING THE DIFFERENCE*

✍

We will not be able to take the positive steps toward the enjoyment marriage was designed to provide until we first take steps to recognize more clearly the selfishness we so easily excuse. —DR. LARRY CRABB, *MEN & WOMEN: ENJOYING THE DIFFERENCE*

❧

A husband's responsibility within his home extends far beyond material provision. God directly commands the husband to love his wife according to the example of one who sacrificed all, including his position, to remove obstacles to relationship that *his bride had created* and to thereby introduce her to an intimacy they could both enjoy. — DR. LARRY CRABB, *MEN & WOMEN: ENJOYING THE DIFFERENCE*

❧

Start each day with pleasant words. Your family will be the first to benefit. . . . Be pleasant in your remarks, cheerful with your greetings. As you are slipping out of bed, thank God for His love . . . His calm, fresh reminders that this new day is under His control. Quietly state the encouraging truth: God loves me. —CHARLES R. SWINDOLL, *GROWING STRONG IN THE SEASONS OF LIFE*

❧

He who finds a wife finds what is good and receives favor from the LORD. —PROVERBS 18:22

❧

Let love and faithfulness never leave you; bind them around your neck, write them on the tablet of your heart. —PROVERBS 3:3

Wisdom For... Your Role As Father

Sons are a heritage from the LORD, children a reward from him. Like arrows in the hands of a warrior are sons born in one's youth. Blessed is the man whose quiver is full of them. They will not be put to shame when they contend with their enemies in the gate. —PSALM 127:3–5

JP

When it comes to rearing children, developing a strong home where happiness and harmony can flourish, there is a primary starting point: *knowing* your child.... Knowing your child takes time, careful observation, diligent study, prayer, concentration, help from above, and, yes, wisdom. —CHARLES R. SWINDOLL, *THE STRONG FAMILY*

JP

Christian parents who truly understand the goal of parenting-to draw out the image-bearing potential of each child-become fully engaged in the challenge.... They do *anything* they can to encourage authentic Christian growth in their children—even if it slows their professional advancement and postpones the pursuit of personal dreams. —BILL HYBELS, *HONEST TO GOD?*

ぷ

Train a child in the way he should go, and when he is old he will not turn from it. —PROVERBS 22:6

ぷ

It is impossible for me to transfer to my child a principle I do not personally embrace, that is, a love for God that permeates all my heart. It is impossible for me to convince my child of the value of honesty . . . if I am dishonest. Impossible for me to convey to my child the necessity of clean lips if I habitually practice profanity. It is impossible for children to grasp the importance of care and compassion for others if their parents run roughshod over others. —CHARLES R. SWINDOLL, *THE STRONG FAMILY*

ぷ

If we fail our children by wielding a sword of ignorance and hatred, cutting down others in a feeble and pathetic attempt to raise ourselves up, we have endangered our future. —MEL BLOUNT, *THE CROSS BURNS BRIGHTLY*

ぷ

Be careful, and watch yourselves closely so that you do not forget the things your eyes have seen or let them

slip from your heart as long as you live. Teach them to your children and to their children after them.
— DEUTERONOMY 4:9

∞

These commandments . . . are to be upon your hearts. Impress them on your children. Talk about them when you sit at home and when you walk along the road, when you lie down and when you get up. . . . Write them on the doorframes of your houses and on your gates.
— DEUTERONOMY 6:6–7,9

∞

God's desire is that there be a conscious, consistent, transfer of God's truth from the older to the younger in the family. If there is an unconscious mistake Christian parents make, it is thinking that our children automatically capture our zeal for Christ. — CHARLES R. SWINDOLL, *THE STRONG FAMILY*

∞

He decreed statutes for Jacob and established the law in Israel, which he commanded our forefathers to teach their children, so the next generation would know them, even the children yet to be born, and they in turn would tell their children. — PSALM 78:5–6

⚜

Each day of our lives we make deposits into the memory banks of our children. By remembering that, I find I am more likely to work on the qualities that build a lasting relationship between my children and me. —CHARLES R. SWINDOLL, *THE STRONG FAMILY*

⚜

What kind of mark are you leaving on your children, especially your sons? Do you realize that your little boys are watching you like hawks? They're trying to figure out what maleness is all about, and you're their model. I hope they see in you a deep, uncompromising love for God. I hope they see both toughness and tenderness. . . . Your little girls, too, will benefit because they'll grow up with a clear vision of the kind of men who make godly husbands. —BILL HYBELS, *HONEST TO GOD?*

⚜

By far the most valuable thing you can give your children is a loving relationship with you, their father. The material possessions you provide are of secondary importance. —PAUL LEWIS, *THE FIVE KEY HABITS OF SMART DADS*

⚜

What often energizes me to choose my kids instead of my work is the fact that I get only one shot at my kids. —PAUL LEWIS, *THE FIVE KEY HABITS OF SMART DADS*

ॐ

Instead of challenging fathers to give of themselves, the system encourages them to give the stuff their increased salaries can buy. . . . Let's remember that the greatest earthly gifts we can provide are our presence and influence while we live and a magnificent memory of our lives once we're gone. — CHARLES R. SWINDOLL, *THE STRONG FAMILY*

ॐ

Because they are fragile, handling children with care is essential. You'll be glad you did when all you have is an old photo and the memory of a package God delivered into your care many, many years ago. — CHARLES R. SWINDOLL, *GROWING STRONG IN THE SEASONS OF LIFE*

ॐ

A hundred years from now the size of my bank account won't matter, nor the size or style house I lived in, nor the model car I drove. But the world may be different because I was deeply involved in the life of my children. — PAUL LEWIS, *THE FIVE KEY HABITS OF SMART DADS*

ॐ

Beyond what it doesn't do for your children, putting all your energy and time into the career basket can set you up for an identity crisis if your career is derailed. . . . Just as you would diversify a financial portfolio, you must balance your life choices to provide security and satisfaction in family relationships. — PAUL LEWIS, *THE FIVE KEY HABITS OF SMART DADS*

❦

Children's children are a crown to the aged, and parents are the pride of their children. — PROVERBS 17:6

❦

The righteous man leads a blameless life; blessed are his children after him. — PROVERBS 20:7

❦

As your father left you a legacy, you also will leave one for your children. When you recognize the imprint of your father on you, you now have a chance to choose your legacy. — PAUL LEWIS, *THE FIVE KEY HABITS OF SMART DADS*

❦

How long has it been since your child has heard you say you were wrong? That you failed? Communication is enhanced when you admit your faults and errors and seek forgiveness. — PAUL LEWIS, *THE FIVE KEY HABITS OF SMART DADS*

❦

The most productive fathering time of your day may be the five minutes you stop along your route home, close your eyes, and determine your family agenda for the evening-especially your first 30 minutes. —PAUL LEWIS, *THE FIVE KEY HABITS OF SMART DADS*

✧

The father of a righteous man has great joy; he who has a wise son delights in him. —PROVERBS 23:24

✧

A godly father is a man who understands what he means to his children, who is humbled by overwhelming joy over the impact he can make for God and terrified by the damage he can do. He is both thrilled and scared. Because of his confidence in God, the thrill is stronger. —DR. LARRY CRABB, *THE SILENCE OF ADAM*

✧

For what are you asking the Lord on behalf of your life and your children? . . . Stop long enough to think it over. And don't just think, get alone and *write down* your thoughts, your dreams, your aspirations. —CHARLES R. SWINDOLL, *GROWING STRONG IN THE SEASONS OF LIFE*

✧

As a father has compassion on his children, so the LORD has compassion on those who fear him. —PSALM 103:13

❧

Is *yours* an encouraging home? If I were to drop by as an invisible guest and listen in on conversations, would I hear sarcasm, put-downs, and caustic comments? Or would I hear, "Good job! I notice you're growing up. What a delight you are to our family." — CHARLES R. SWINDOLL, *GROWING DEEP*

❧

Safer, more satisfying fathering comes easier as you move slowly. Don't hurry your children to grow up too soon. Let each grow at his or her appropriate pace. Don't rush yourself, either. Take time to develop the skills, knowledge, and habits that allow you to father your children well. — PAUL LEWIS, *THE FIVE KEY HABITS OF SMART DADS*

❧

We are to model God's place of authority until our children are sufficiently mature to shift the authority from us to their heavenly Parent. — CHARLES R. SWINDOLL, *THE STRONG FAMILY*

❧

Children are a lot like chickens . . . they need room to squawk, lay a few eggs, flap their wings, even to fly the coop. Otherwise, let me warn you, all that lid-sitting will one day explode and you'll wish you had not taken such a protective stance. — CHARLES R. SWINDOLL, *THE STRONG FAMILY*

❧

Fathers, do not exasperate your children; instead, bring them up in the training and instruction of the Lord. —Ephesians 6:4

❧

Do not withhold discipline from a child; if you punish him with the rod, he will not die. Punish him with the rod and save his soul from death. —Proverbs 23:13–14

❧

Often it's just forgetting commonsense prevention that gets dads into fathering trouble. If you don't practice preventive fathering, you'll end up playing catch-up or trying to compensate for an outright mistake you made earlier. —Paul Lewis, *The Five Key Habits of Smart Dads*

❧

Rather than causing your child to question your love, discipline *confirms* your love. . . . When you care enough to set healthy limits, take the time to enforce the rules, and model the things you expect, children grow up much happier and more secure than those who are given virtually free rein. —Charles R. Swindoll, *The Strong Family*

❧

He who spares the rod hates his son, but he who loves him is careful to discipline him. —Proverbs 13:24

* SP *

The rod of correction imparts wisdom, but a child left to himself disgraces his mother. . . . Discipline your son, and he will give you peace; he will bring delight to your soul. —PROVERBS 29:15,17

SP

The world outside the family circle is dark enough. When the light goes out *within* the circle . . . how great is the darkness. . . . Too many of us are beginning to resemble stern-faced East German guards patrolling the wall rather than approachable, believable parents, building happy memories. —CHARLES R. SWINDOLL, *GROWING STRONG IN THE SEASONS OF LIFE*

SP

As long as your children are alive, it is never too late to start developing habits of loving, approving, and encouraging your child—never too late to start cheering. —PAUL LEWIS, *THE FIVE KEY HABITS OF SMART DADS*

SP

I can't do anything about my ancestors, but I can do a lot about my descendants. —PAUL LEWIS, THE FIVE KEY HABITS OF SMART DADS

❧

All your sons will be taught by the LORD, and great will be your children's peace. —ISAIAH 54:13

❧

"Where your treasure is," noted Jesus Christ, "there your heart will be also." If I find my significance—my treasure—primarily in my work, that's where my attention and my time will be focused. Yet when I have grasped my significance as a father, I will treasure *that* role and opportunity increasingly. —PAUL LEWIS, *THE FIVE KEY HABITS OF SMART DADS*

❧

There are numerous lessons to be learned from hard work. Happy is the family who has a model of diligence in the man of the home. And *happier* is the family when dad keeps the right perspective on his diligence.
—CHARLES R. SWINDOLL, *THE STRONG FAMILY*

❧

It is easy to let things you buy for your family take the place of giving yourself. In our affluent era, how easy to provide too much too soon! —CHARLES R. SWINDOLL, *THE STRONG FAMILY*

❧

A greedy man brings trouble to his family, but he who hates bribes will live. —PROVERBS 15:27

∽

When it comes to the Christian family, isn't the gospel *alone* enough? *Absolutely not!* To hear the gospel is a necessity for children. If they are to come to know the Savior whom you love, Dad, they need to have you tell them of Him. — CHARLES R. SWINDOLL, *THE STRONG FAMILY*

∽

The greatest sin that results from people's fighting with one another is the trouble that we make for our children. I believe that we adults should see ourselves as the champions, caretakers, and defenders of children. They have no vote, no voice, no rights to speak of; they only have us to protect them. — MEL BLOUNT, *THE CROSS BURNS BRIGHTLY*

∽

Fathers, do not embitter your children, or they will become discouraged. — COLOSSIANS 3:21

∽

Do not try to force your child to fulfill what was never fulfilled in *your* life. . . . Wise are the parents who train up their children according to the way God has put them together. — CHARLES R. SWINDOLL, *THE STRONG FAMILY*

☙

The best parenting strategy is a difficult one: take note of your child's talents and adapt your training methods to mesh with the child's style. —PAUL LEWIS, *THE FIVE KEY HABITS OF SMART DADS*

☙

God numbers the hairs on my head, Jesus taught, and a sparrow cannot fall to the ground without his knowing. That kind of all-knowing and caring God can coach a father to maximize his moments and number his days with his children. —PAUL LEWIS, *THE FIVE KEY HABITS OF SMART DADS*

Wisdom For . . . Being A Godly Man

God created man in his own image, in the image of God he created him; male and female he created them.
— GENESIS 1:27

∂∫∂

The separate distinction of male and female is not merely a "traditional expectation," it's a biblical precept ("male and female He created them," Genesis 1:27b). And . . . it is a foundational block upon which any healthy civilization rests. When the roles get sufficiently blurred, confusion and chaos replace decency and order.
— CHARLES R. SWINDOLL, *THE STRONG FAMILY*

∂∫∂

Genuine masculinity requires that individual men be "man enough" to admit their need for a vital relationship with the true God. They must make God their number one priority. — BILL HYBELS, *HONEST TO GOD?*

❧

Blessed is the man who does not walk in the counsel of the wicked or stand in the way of sinners or sit in the seat of mockers. But his delight is in the law of the LORD, and on his law he meditates day and night. —PSALM 1:1–2

❧

Trust in the LORD with all your heart and lean not on your own understanding; in all your ways acknowledge him, and he will make your paths straight. —PROVERBS 3:5–6

❧

We must act on the promise that God can do all things through Christ who strengthens us. It sounds impossible. Scary. Some of us would rather walk into a raging river than do what we need to do. But God promises power along the way. —BILL HYBELS, *DESCENDING INTO GREATNESS*

❧

Those who become so strong that they feel no need of God will ultimately get their wish, but not as they imagined. Their "glory" will be turned into shame, and their great power will be powerless to save them. But those who are "weak," who humbly admit their need for God's help and daily strength, will find that they have been granted the only power that matters—the power of God. —JACK KUHATSCHEK, *THE SUPERMAN SYNDROME*

❧

A man is "manly" when he moves through life with a purposeful and confident involvement, when he follows a direction that he values for reasons that are bigger than himself. — DR. LARRY CRABB, *MEN & WOMEN: ENJOYING THE DIFFERENCE*

❧

Be on your guard; stand firm in the faith; be men of courage; be strong. Do everything in love. — 1 CORINTHIANS 16:13–14

❧

Don't try to prove yourself by being macho. In all your relationships, learn to mix strength with sensitivity, toughness with tenderness, leadership with submission. — BILL HYBELS, *HONEST TO GOD?*

❧

The head of every man is Christ, and the head of the woman is man, and the head of Christ is God. . . . In the Lord, however, woman is not independent of man, nor is man independent of woman. For as woman came from man, so also man is born of woman. But everything comes from God. — 1 CORINTHIANS 11:3,11–12

❧

Men who spend their lives finding God are quietly transformed from mere men into elders: *godly men* who know what it means to trust a person when there is no plan to follow; *spiritual fathers* who enter dark caves that their children run from; *Christlike mentors* who speak into that darkness with strength instead of control, with gentleness instead of destructive force, and with wisdom that cuts through the confusion to the beauty beyond. — DR. LARRY CRABB, *THE SILENCE OF ADAM*

❧

The right kind of toughness-strength of character— ought to mark the man of today . . . but not only that. Tenderness—gentleness—is equally important.
— CHARLES R. SWINDOLL, *GROWING STRONG IN THE SEASONS OF LIFE*

❧

Our goal is balance . . . always balance. . . . Not just *tough*. That alone makes a man cold, distant, intolerant, unbearable. But tough *and* tender . . . gentle, thoughtful, teachable, considerate. — CHARLES R. SWINDOLL, *GROWING STRONG IN THE SEASONS OF LIFE*

❧

But the fruit of the Spirit is love, joy, peace, patience, kindness, goodness, faithfulness, gentleness and self-control. — GALATIANS 5:22–23a

ఆసా

It is to a man's honor to avoid strife, but every fool is quick to quarrel. — PROVERBS 20:3

ఆసా

It can be argued that men today tend to be more relationally sensitive than our stern forefathers. Perhaps we are more aware of "connecting" with our wives, children, and friends. . . . But whatever gains we have made in modern society have been largely stripped of their value, because most of us have lost the depth of connection with Christ that only comes through unexplained suffering, excruciating brokenness, and deep repentance. — DR. LARRY CRABB, *THE SILENCE OF ADAM*

ఆసా

God wants men to be free to demonstrate tenderness, sensitivity, understanding, meekness, and humility. Free to be vulnerable enough to foster intimacy and to shed tears. — BILL HYBELS, *HONEST TO GOD?*

ఆసా

Thank you for that shortest but sweetest verse in all the Bible—"Jesus wept." Thank you for those tears you cried so openly. They have given not only dignity to my grief but freedom to my emotions. — KEN GIRE, *INCREDIBLE MOMENTS WITH THE SAVIOR*

ॐ

The Lord takes note of our inner friction when hard times are oiled by tears. He turns these situations into moments of tenderness; He never forgets those crises in our lives where tears were shed. — CHARLES R. SWINDOLL, *GROWING STRONG IN THE SEASONS OF LIFE*

ॐ

The LORD's unfailing love surrounds the man who trusts in him. — PSALM 32:10b

ॐ

God wants us all to experience a deeper level of security. He wants emasculated men to become secure enough to confront timidity and fear, to take risks and make commitments. He wants macho men to become secure enough to crawl out from under the false pretensions and quit trying to impress people. — BILL HYBELS, *HONEST TO GOD?*

ॐ

Males need to be contrite enough to admit their need for God, yet courageous enough to step out in faith. It's no small thing to admit personal sin and seek a Savior. — BILL HYBELS, *HONEST TO GOD?*

❧

The fear of the LORD teaches a man wisdom, and humility comes before honor. —PROVERBS 15:33

❧

Blessed is the man who fears the LORD, who finds great delight in his commands. His children will be mighty in the land; the generation of the upright will be blessed. —PSALM 112:1–2

❧

God calls a man to speak into darkness, to remember who God is and what he has revealed about life, and—with that memory uppermost in his mind—to move into his relationships and responsibilities with the imaginative strength of Christ. —DR. LARRY CRABB, *THE SILENCE OF ADAM*

❧

Who, then, is the man that fears the LORD? He will instruct him in the way chosen for him. He will spend his days in prosperity, and his descendants will inherit the land. —PSALM 25:12–13

❧

Develop and maintain a vital relationship with God. Make it the driving priority in your life. Don't apologize for it, or view it as a sign of weakness. Be strong enough to be completely devoted to God. —BILL HYBELS, *HONEST TO GOD?*

❧

When we are properly motivated, we are released to accomplish more. We are also less vulnerable to the doubt and guilt that strangle so many. . . . There is only one motivation that will take you to the ultimate freedom that God intended for your life: a passionate love for God. — KEN DAVIS, *FIRE UP YOUR LIFE!*

❧

Religious men of today too often have found a convenient God, an immediately useful God promoted by leaders who are filled more by the thrill of adoring crowds than by their opportunity for quiet communion with God. — DR. LARRY CRABB, *THE SILENCE OF ADAM*

❧

What is your purpose for living? . . . The greatest and most productive purpose is to live to fulfill *God's* purpose for your life—to follow the manufacturer's recommendations for peak performance, to continue to press toward the mark of his high calling. — KEN DAVIS, *FIRE UP YOUR LIFE!*

❧

To man belong the plans of the heart, but from the LORD comes the reply. . . . Commit to the LORD whatever you do, and your plans will succeed. — PROVERBS 16:1,3

❧

To dream is an audacious act of faith. It is the ability to endow the heart with the gift of vision. It is believing in the substance of things we can only hope for, the evidence of things we cannot see. Dare to dream. Help your children dream. Reach out and take the dream God has for you. — WINTLEY PHIPPS, *THE POWER OF A DREAM*

❧

Many are the plans in a man's heart, but it is the LORD's purpose that prevails. — PROVERBS 19:21

❧

Even when God leads you through difficult times, you won't find a more fulfilling life than the one you can live right in the center of God's will. — KEN DAVIS, *FIRE UP YOUR LIFE!*

❧

Abraham was expected to go where God led him, a step at a time, a day at a time. There were no guarantees that the journey would be easy. He had a lot of heartache along the way, his share of danger, and the painful introspection of living with postponed hopes. Yet he is remembered as a man of faith. — DAVE & JAN DRAVECKY, *WHEN YOU CAN'T COME BACK*

✌

A man is most manly when he admits "I don't know what to do in this situation, but I know it's important that I get involved and do something. I will therefore envision what God may want to see happen in this person's life or in this circumstance, and I will move toward that vision with whatever wisdom and power God supplies me." A manly man moves even when there are no recipes. — DR. LARRY CRABB, *THE SILENCE OF ADAM*

✌

Our Creator . . . knows that only he is capable of meeting even our most basic of needs. He doesn't want us to miss today's blessing because we are clinging to some worthless morsel, worried about how we will survive tomorrow. — KEN DAVIS, *FIRE UP YOUR LIFE!*

✌

It's impossible to live victoriously for Christ without courage. That's why God's thrice-spoken command to Joshua is as timeless as it is true: "Be strong and courageous!" (Joshua 1:6,7,9). Are you? Honestly now— are you? Or are you quick to quit . . . ready to run when the heat rises? — CHARLES R. SWINDOLL, *GROWING STRONG IN THE SEASONS OF LIFE*

৵৶

Flog a mocker, and the simple will learn prudence; rebuke a discerning man, and he will gain knowledge. —Proverbs 19:25

৵৶

Focus your full attention on one of the rarest of all virtues. It is a virtue that everybody pursues, but very few possess on a regular basis. I'm referring to the often-longed-for but seldom-found virtue of peace. —Charles R. Swindoll, *Stress Fractures*

৵৶

Consider the blameless, observe the upright; there is a future for the man of peace. —Psalm 37:37

৵৶

Divine power is not mediated through strength, but through weakness; . . . true greatness is not achieved through the assertion of rights, but through their release; . . . even the most secular of things can be sacred when you are in their midst. —Ken Gire, *Intimate Moments With The Savior*

৵৶

The more a man understands a woman and is controlled by a Spirit-prompted other-centered commitment to bless her, the more "masculine" he becomes. And he will become more masculine in an unself-conscious fashion. — DR. LARRY CRABB, *MEN & WOMEN: ENJOYING THE DIFFERENCE*

❧

God wants men to be free. Free to demonstrate toughness when a situation or relationship demands it. Free to display grit, strength, tenacity, commitment, and decisiveness under the Holy Spirit's direction. — BILL HYBELS, *HONEST TO GOD?*

❧

A man of knowledge uses words with restraint, and a man of understanding is even-tempered. — PROVERBS 17:27

❧

Do not envy a violent man or choose any of his ways, for the LORD detests a perverse man but takes the upright into his confidence. — PROVERBS 3:31–32

❧

Whenever *any* of God's children become proud, you can be sure that something will happen to humble them and bring their head back to normal size. — JACK KUHATSCHEK, *THE SUPERMAN SYNDROME*

಄ೆಔ

What is your final authority in life? What holds you together when all hell breaks loose around you? There can be no more reliable authority on earth than God's Word, the Bible. This timeless, trustworthy source of truth holds the key that unlocks life's mysteries. It alone provides us with the shelter we need in times of storm. —CHARLES R. SWINDOLL, *GROWING DEEP*

಄ೆಔ

Life is literally filled with God-appointed storms. . . . Two things should comfort us in the midst of daily lightning and thunder and rain and wind. First, these squalls surge across *everyone's* horizon. . . . Second, we all *need* them. . . . The massive blows and shattering blasts . . . smooth us, humble us, and compel us to submit to *His* script and *His* chosen role for our lives. —CHARLES R. SWINDOLL, *GROWING STRONG IN THE SEASONS OF LIFE*

಄ೆಔ

All of life is a blessing . . . the Lord is with us even if we falter, He is with us even if we fail, He is with us when we break, and He can help to make us whole. —DENNIS BYRD, *RISE & WALK: THE TRIAL & TRIUMPH OF DENNIS BYRD*

಄ೆಔ

God brings about birthdays . . . not as deadlines but *lifelines*. He builds them into our calendar once every year to enable us to make an annual appraisal, not only of our length of life but our depth. Not simply to tell us we're growing older . . . but to help us determine if we are also growing deeper. —CHARLES R. SWINDOLL, *GROWING STRONG IN THE SEASONS OF LIFE*

అ

Men who learn to be fascinated more with Christ than with themselves will become the authentic men of our day. Men of this generation must learn to count the cost of following Christ (the cost is easily calculated: everything we have); we must feel the emptiness of our souls until no cost seems too high if it brings us into contact with him; . . . To put it simply, we must be more concerned with knowing Christ than with finding ourselves. —DR. LARRY CRABB, *THE SILENCE OF ADAM*

Wisdom For . . . Being A Friend

To have friends we must *be* friendly. Friendliness is a matter of being someone . . . more than it is doing something. —CHARLES R. SWINDOLL, *GROWING STRONG IN THE SEASONS OF LIFE*

❦

A friend loves at all times. —PROVERBS 17:17a

❦

Do not forsake your friend and the friend of your father. —PROVERBS 27:10

❦

We must prayerfully seek a man to be our brother. But even more, we must prayerfully seek to be a brother for another man.

There is an untapped reservoir of power in Christian community. Some of that power will only be released when men become brothers. —DR. LARRY CRABB, *THE SILENCE OF ADAM*

❧

God offered us His love without considering whether we deserved it or not; we are called to offer love in exactly the same way. Or, in the words of Paul, "in humility consider others more important than yourselves." —BILL HYBELS, *DESCENDING INTO GREATNESS*

❧

Be completely humble and gentle; be patient, bearing with one another in love. Make every effort to keep the unity of the Spirit through the bond of peace. —EPHESIANS 4:2–3

❧

When someone betrays me, grant me such a forgiving heart that I would offer a kind word in exchange for a deceitful kiss.

When danger surrounds me, grant me such faithfulness for my friends that I would think of their welfare before my own. —KEN GIRE, *INCREDIBLE MOMENTS WITH THE SAVIOR*

❧

If anyone wants to be first, he must be the very last, and the servant of all. —MARK 9:35

⁂

Service, believe it or not, is the way we operate best—the way we were *designed* to operate. In our relationship with God and with our fellow man, a spirit of sacrifice and compassion leads to abundant life. — KEN DAVIS, *FIRE UP YOUR LIFE!*

⁂

Do to others as you would have them do to you. . . . Do not judge, and you will not be judged. Do not condemn, and you will not be condemned. Forgive, and you will be forgiven. Give, and it will be given to you. —LUKE 6:31,37–38

⁂

Each day the Spirit calls us to follow, to descend: to call and encourage a friend, . . . reconcile a relationship, ask forgiveness, admonish a friend—to make ourselves nothing so we can love better. —BILL HYBELS, *DESCENDING INTO GREATNESS*

⁂

Encourage one another and build each other up, just as in fact you are doing. —1 THESSALONIANS 5:11

❦

It is impossible to stimulate someone else to love and good deeds if we are not around them. We cannot be an encouragement if we live our lives in secret caves, pushing people away from us. People out of touch don't encourage others. Encouragement is a face-to-face thing. . . . *Encouragement is not the responsibility of a gifted few, but the responsibility of all in the family of God.* —CHARLES R. SWINDOLL, *GROWING DEEP*

❦

Busyness rapes relationships. It substitutes shallow frenzy for deep friendship. —CHARLES R. SWINDOLL, *GROWING STRONG IN THE SEASONS OF LIFE*

❦

Carry each other's burdens, and in this way you will fulfill the law of Christ. —GALATIANS 6:2

❦

We desperately need the help that can come through listening to one another. We do not need to be trained psychoanalysts to be trained listeners. The most important requirements are compassion and patience. —RICHARD J. FOSTER, *CELEBRATION OF DISCIPLINE*

* જ્ર*

Comfort for the sorrowing cannot be regulated and systematized.... *Be real.* As you reach out, admit your honest feelings to your friends.... *Be quiet.* Your presence, not your words, will be most appreciated.... *Be supportive.* Those who comfort must have a tender heart of understanding.... *Be available....* Be committed to comforting later on as well as now. —CHARLES R. SWINDOLL, *GROWING STRONG IN THE SEASONS OF LIFE*

* જ્ર*

Now that you have purified yourselves by obeying the truth so that you have sincere love for your brothers, love one another deeply, from the heart. —1 PETER 1:22

* જ્ર*

Keep on loving each other as brothers. —HEBREWS 13:1

જ્ર

My command is this: Love each other as I have loved you. Greater love has no one than this, that he lay down his life for his friends. You are my friends if you do what I command. —JOHN 15:12–14

* જ્ર*

Anybody can tell you what a world this would be
  If we learned to love each other.
I know we would see it, sharing what's in our hearts.

We learn to live together through the stormy
    weather.
No matter how hard we try.
We've got to keep believing we can make a
    better world.

— WINTLEY PHIPPS, *THE POWER OF A DREAM*

ঞ

Help me to be a friend who loves as you did at that
Last Supper—a friend who loves to the end, even when
that love is refused. — KEN GIRE, *INTIMATE MOMENTS WITH THE
SAVIOR*

ঞ

Love is most perfectly fulfilled when we bear the
hurts and sufferings of each other, weeping with those
who weep. — RICHARD J. FOSTER, *CELEBRATION OF DISCIPLINE*

ঞ

Shine a light in someone's life;
    try to make a difference.
Reach down inside your heart,
    show you really care.
Someone may find in you hope
    for their tomorrow,
And all you did was smile.
It will make you feel God put you there.
You'll believe that you can really.

— WINTLEY PHIPPS, *THE POWER OF A DREAM*

❦

Clothe yourselves with compassion, kindness, humility, gentleness and patience. Bear with each other and forgive whatever grievances you may have against one another. Forgive as the Lord forgave you. And over all these virtues put on love, which binds them all together in perfect unity. —COLOSSIANS 3:12b–14

❦

Above all, love each other deeply, because love covers over a multitude of sins. —1 PETER 4:8

❦

Transforming faith, the Bible tells us, happens only in the context of movement. The power of God comes to those who obey. And obedience means taking action—to love one another, to restore a relationship, to confront a person in sin. God promises to give us power as we act. —BILL HYBELS, *DESCENDING INTO GREATNESS*

❦

Ask God to give you the ability to be positive, honest, and open (and comfortable doing so!) at all times. Ask Him to use you to *be* a friend to someone who is needing a friend. —CHARLES R. SWINDOLL, *GROWING STRONG IN THE SEASONS OF LIFE*

ఎఓ

We need to give one another stretching space—the room to respond and react in a variety of ways, even as our infinite Creator molded a variety of personalities. . . . So instead of biting and devouring one another (Galatians 5:15), let's support individual freedom as we serve one another in love (Galatians 5:13). — CHARLES R. SWINDOLL, *GROWING STRONG IN THE SEASONS OF LIFE*

ఎఓ

You, my brothers, were called to be free. But do not use your freedom to indulge the sinful nature; rather, serve one another in love. — GALATIANS 5:13

ఎఓ

If you keep on biting and devouring each other, watch out or you will be destroyed by each other. — GALATIANS 5:15

ఎఓ

A healthy attitude toward ourselves is necessary before there can be a healthy attitude towards others . . . and attract them as friends. — CHARLES R. SWINDOLL, *GROWING STRONG IN THE SEASONS OF LIFE*

❧

The only escape from indifference is to think of people as our most cherished resource. We need to work hard at . . . people involvement, . . . nonsuperficial conversations, times when we genuinely get involved with folks in need—not *just* pray for them. —CHARLES R. SWINDOLL, GROWING STRONG IN THE SEASONS OF LIFE

❧

He who covers over an offense promotes love, but whoever repeats the matter separates close friends. —PROVERBS 17:9

❧

Over the years I've heard many people complain about the lack of genuine fellowship in the church. But I've never heard that complaint made by someone who's involved in authentic service. Service draws people together in the pursuit of common goals. That inevitably opens the door to significant relationships. —BILL HYBELS, HONEST TO GOD?

❧

Two are better than one, because they have a good return for their work: If one falls down, his friend can help him up. But pity the man who falls and has no one to help him up! —ECCLESIASTES 4:9–10

෴

The pleasantness of one's friend springs from his earnest counsel. —PROVERBS 27:9b

෴

Do you have a friend or friends—preferably of the same sex—who hold you accountable on a regular basis? It's easy to mentally agree with the concept of accountability, but it takes determination (dare I say "guts?") to follow through and *do* something about it. —CHARLES R. SWINDOLL, *THE BRIDE*

෴

Better is open rebuke than hidden love. Wounds from a friend can be trusted, but an enemy multiplies kisses. —PROVERBS 27:5–6

෴

Before your lips start moving, pause ten seconds and mentally preview your words. Are they accurate or exaggerated? Kind or cutting? . . . *Talk less.* . . . Compulsive talkers find it difficult to keep friends. They're irritating. So conserve your verbal energy! —CHARLES R. SWINDOLL, *GROWING STRONG IN THE SEASONS OF LIFE*

❧

Most of us give off an air of being on top of things. We're winning: We've got life by the tail. We can handle it. And so we give superficial comments to people, and we respond superficially in return, . . . and that doesn't bring encouragement. — CHARLES R. SWINDOLL, *GROWING DEEP*

❧

We often think we should mask the truth of our past lest people think less of us—especially if our today is much more respectable than our yesterday. But the truth is, when we peel off our masks, others are usually not repelled; they are drawn closer to us. — CHARLES R. SWINDOLL, *GROWING STRONG IN THE SEASONS OF LIFE*

❧

If we walk in the light, as he is in the light, we have fellowship with one another, and the blood of Jesus, his Son, purifies us from all sin. — 1 JOHN 1:7

❧

Make every effort to add to your faith goodness; and to goodness, knowledge; and to knowledge, self-control; and to self-control, perseverance; and to perseverance, godliness; and to godliness, brotherly kindness; and to brotherly kindness, love. — 2 PETER 1:5–7

ఎ❧

If we genuinely desire some depth to emerge, some impact to be made, some profound and enduring investment to cast a comforting shadow across another's life . . . it is essential that we slow down . . . at times, stop completely. And think. Now . . . not later. Don't you dare put this off another day! — CHARLES R. SWINDOLL, *GROWING STRONG IN THE SEASONS OF LIFE*

ఎ❧

We must never wait until we *feel* like praying before we pray for others. Prayer is like any other work; we may not feel like working, but once we have been at it for a bit, we begin to feel like working. — RICHARD J. FOSTER, *CELEBRATION OF DISCIPLINE*

ఎ❧

Dear friends, let us love one another, for love comes from God. Everyone who loves has been born of God and knows God. — 1 JOHN 4:7

ఎ❧

A man of many companions may come to ruin, but there is a friend who sticks closer than a brother. — PROVERBS 18:24

❧

Sometimes character takes a more active role . . . such as doing something exceptional when it is not expected—sacrificing your own comfort, time, safety, even your life for a greater good. . . . Putting others first, regardless of what it may cost, demonstrates the deepest virtues of the human character. — D. JAMES KENNEDY, *CHARACTER & DESTINY*

❧

Eusebius tells us that when they were putting Peter on the cross, he asked to be crucified upside down for he didn't feel worthy to die in the same manner his Lord had. What kind of friend inspires devotion like that? A friend who prayed for him when he was weak. A friend who forgave him when he failed. A friend who healed a painful memory. A friend who loved him. A friend who believed in him. A friend like Jesus. —KEN GIRE, *INTIMATE MOMENTS WITH THE SAVIOR*

Wisdom For . . . The Workplace

I realized it is good and proper for a man to eat and drink, and to find satisfaction in his toilsome labor under the sun during the few days of life God has given him—for this is his lot. Moreover, when God gives any man wealth and possessions, and enables him to enjoy them, to accept his lot and be happy in his work—this is a gift of God. —ECCLESIASTES 5:18–19

✑

Don't be afraid of work. In fact, don't settle for anything less than the best. . . . As Christians we have not only a different motive for excellence but also a different standard of excellence. True excellence is not measured by greater profits and increased dividends; it is not measured by market shares and customer satisfaction. Our motive and standard for excellence is the Lord Jesus Christ. —WINTLEY PHIPPS, THE POWER OF A DREAM

❧

Remember the LORD your God, for it is he who gives you the ability to produce wealth, and so confirms his covenant, which he swore to your forefathers, as it is today. —DEUTERONOMY 8:18

❧

Honor the LORD with your wealth, with the firstfruits of all your crops; then your barns will be filled to over-flowing, and your vats will brim over with new wine. —PROVERBS 3:9-10

❧

Why would a loving God put His children to work as soon as He created them? Because He knew human labor was a blessing. He knew it would provide them challenges, excitement, adventure, and rewards that nothing else would. He knew that creatures made in His image needed to devote their time to meaningful tasks. —BILL HYBELS, HONEST TO GOD?

❧

Human labor was designed by God, assigned to every one of us, and offered as an opportunity to build confidence, develop character, and enjoy the satisfaction of accomplishment. —BILL HYBELS, HONEST TO GOD?

❧

The fine art of working is a lost art today—really getting in there and studying the job, reading and expanding your knowledge. Becoming an expert in your field—for the simple delight of accomplishment! —CHARLES R. SWINDOLL, *GROWING STRONG IN THE SEASONS OF LIFE*

❧

Whatever you do, whether in word or deed, do it all in the name of the Lord Jesus, giving thanks to God the Father through him. —COLOSSIANS 3:17

❧

When a Christian walks on the job site he should be thinking about more than making money, impressing the boss, or even how much he enjoys his work. He should be conjuring up ways to honor God through his marketplace endeavors. —BILL HYBELS, *HONEST TO GOD?*

❧

Usually we're so busy with our tasks, we forget that above all else, what our people get from us is *us*—our values, our attitudes, our perceptions. In the long run, it's not our skills or our know-how or our long experience that makes the biggest impact—*we* are the main message! How do you share yourself through your work? —DON SHULA & KEN BLANCHARD, *EVERYONE'S A COACH*

❧

What kind of mark are you leaving in your businesses, government, schools, and churches? The future of our nation will be bright if it can be passed on to a generation of young men who love God deeply and have the humility and confidence to lead wisely. —BILL HYBELS, *HONEST TO GOD?*

❧

Make it your ambition to lead a quiet life, to mind your own business and to work with your hands, just as we told you, so that your daily life may win the respect of outsiders and so that you will not be dependent on anybody. —1 THESSALONIANS 4:11–12

❧

Into our screwed-up, twisted, dog-eat-dog world, He wants us to bring humility and servanthood. They will know you are My followers, He said, if you love one another. He didn't include a footnote or a loophole that limits our responsibility to those above us on the Pecking Order. He said to love one another. Period. With no qualifiers attached. —BILL HYBELS, *DESCENDING INTO GREATNESS*

❧

If we can find the courage to trust God to enable us to live lives of service, not only will we begin to move closer to our fullest potential but our families, friends, and

business associates will look at us in a different light.
— KEN DAVIS, *FIRE UP YOUR LIFE!*

❧

Christians ... are those who roll up their sleeves to advance God's kingdom. They give themselves away in love, so God and others might receive. They make decisions not on the basis of economic, social, or status factors, but with only one question in mind: Does this bring God's kingdom on earth closer to reality? — BILL HYBELS, *DESCENDING INTO GREATNESS*

❧

Do not store up for yourselves treasure on earth, where moth and rust destroy, and where thieves break in and steal. But store up for yourselves treasure in heaven. ... For where your treasure is, there your heart will be also. — MATTHEW 6:19–21

❧

God has a problem with the world's approach to greatness. He knows that self-indulgence, by its very nature, always leads to self-destruction. What seems like a climb to the top, to a deep sense of self-fulfillment, turns out to be the digging of one's own grave. Up, in God's dictionary, always leads down. — BILL HYBELS, *DESCENDING INTO GREATNESS*

჻

Too many people today have traded their faith in the "eternal verities" for the cheap substitute of "material possessions," and, as a consequence, the citizens of this nation have compromised both their character and their soul. —D. JAMES KENNEDY, *CHARACTER & DESTINY*

჻

Measure your life—not by man's measurements but by God's measurements. Measure your life by your eternal investments. You can't afford to neglect them. —WESLEY L. DUEWEL, *MEASURE YOUR LIFE*

჻

No servant can serve two masters. Either he will hate the one and love the other, or he will be devoted to the one and despise the other. You cannot serve both God and Money. —LUKE 16:13

჻

Whoever trusts in his riches will fall, but the righteous will thrive like a green leaf. —PROVERBS 11:28

჻

Do not trust in extortion or take pride in stolen goods; though your riches increase, do not set your heart on them. —PSALMS 62:10

❦

Jesus speaks to the question of economics more than any other single social issue. If, in a comparatively simple society, our Lord lays such strong emphasis upon the spiritual dangers of wealth, how much more should we who live in a highly affluent culture take seriously the economic question. —RICHARD J. FOSTER, *CELEBRATION OF DISCIPLINE*

❦

The first step in breaking the sinister power of money is to pursue a more vital relationship with Jesus Christ. People who walk with Him on a consistent, daily basis make an amazing discovery: He satisfies their soul at its deepest level. As they experience this, they find less and less need to ease the pain in their souls with the temporary anesthetics money can buy. — BILL HYBELS, *HONEST TO GOD?*

❦

Grant that love so pure would change my life. That it would loosen my grip on material things. That it would free me from serving two masters. That it would help me to serve—and love—only you. —KEN GIRE, *INTIMATE MOMENTS WITH THE SAVIOR*

❦

For the love of money is a root of all kinds of evil. Some people, eager for money, have wandered from the

faith and pierced themselves with many griefs.
— 1 TIMOTHY 6:10

כֿ

Help me to understand that only a few things really *are* necessary in life. And when you get right down to it, only one: to sit at your feet . . . listening . . . looking into your eyes . . . and loving you. —KEN GIRE, *INTIMATE MOMENTS WITH THE SAVIOR*

כֿ

Most goals (I want to own a house, I want to be promoted to manager, I want to be a community leader) are too small and confining to be worthy of an entire life. They can easily be thwarted by circumstance. . . . If you want to get the most out of life, it is essential that you first discover a purpose worth living for. —KEN DAVIS, *FIRE UP YOUR LIFE!*

כֿ

Godliness with contentment is great gain. For we brought nothing into the world, and we can take nothing out of it. — 1 TIMOTHY 6:6–7

כֿ

Honest scales and balances are from the LORD; all the weights in the bag are of his making. —PROVERBS 16:11

❧

The biblical injunctions against the exploitation of the poor and the accumulation of wealth are clear and straightforward. ... Jesus declared war on the materialism of his day. (And I would suggest that he declares war on the materialism of our day as well.) —RICHARD J. FOSTER, *CELEBRATION OF DISCIPLINE*

❧

Keep money and possessions in perspective. Although the world shouts that money and fame will bring you fulfillment, don't believe the lies. Wealth and fame are fleeting pleasures, at best. The only lasting joy comes from following God's dream for you. —WINTLEY PHIPPS, *THE POWER OF A DREAM*

❧

Whoever loves money never has money enough; whoever loves wealth is never satisfied with his income. —ECCLESIASTES 5:10a

❧

Help me, O Light of the World, to see all my possessions illumined by your presence. And to remember that their true worth is only in proportion to how they honor you. So teach me to value all you have entrusted to my care in the short life I have on this earth. —KEN GIRE, *INTIMATE MOMENTS WITH THE SAVIOR*

ುಲ

Teach me that life is more than the things necessary to sustain it. Help me to learn that if life is more than food, surely it is more important than how the dining room looks; if it's more than clothes, certainly it is more important than whether there's enough closet space to hold them. — KEN GIRE, *INSTRUCTIVE MOMENTS WITH THE SAVIOR*

ುಲ

God's dream for you is more than comfort, success, or earthly security. God's ultimate dream for you is to become more like his Son, Jesus Christ. — WINTLEY PHIPPS, *THE POWER OF A DREAM*

ುಲ

Blessed are all who fear the LORD, who walk in his ways. You will eat the fruit of your labor; blessings and prosperity will be yours. — PSALM 128:1–2

ುಲ

Lazy hands make a man poor, but diligent hands bring wealth. — PROVERBS 10:4

ುಲ

In neither the Old nor New Testament is laziness smiled upon, especially laziness that is rationalized because one believes in the soon-coming of Christ. Our

Lord frowns on the lack of discipline and diligence. He smiles on a well-ordered private life. He is pleased with the wise use of our time and the proper handling of our possessions. —CHARLES R. SWINDOLL, *GROWING DEEP*

❧

Christian workers should epitomize character qualities like self-discipline, perseverance, and initiative. They should be self-motivated, prompt, organized, and industrious. Their efforts should result in work of the very highest quality. . . . Paul tells us to do our work "with all our hearts"—with energy and excellence. That's the first step in honoring God in our work. —BILL HYBELS, *HONEST TO GOD?*

❧

Slaves, obey your earthly masters in everything; and do it, not only when their eye is on you and to win their favor, but with sincerity of heart and reverence for the Lord. Whatever you do, work at it with all your heart, as working for the Lord, not for men, since you know that you will receive an inheritance from the Lord as a reward. It is the Lord Christ you are serving. —COLOSSIANS 3:22–24

❧

For even when we were with you, we gave you this rule: "If a man will not work, he shall not eat." —2 THESSALONIANS 3:10

ঞ্চ

Consistency... It reveals itself in faithful employees who show up on time, roll up their sleeves, and commit themselves more to doing the job than watching the clock. Diligence is its brother . . . dependability its partner . . . discipline, its parent. — CHARLES R. SWINDOLL, *GROWING STRONG IN THE SEASONS OF LIFE*

ঞ্চ

Wherever we work, whatever our job description, our ultimate boss is Jesus Christ. He's the one we need to please. When we do, our work becomes a source of worship. Our job site becomes a temple. Each project we undertake becomes an offering to God. — BILL HYBELS, *HONEST TO GOD?*

ঞ্চ

The very best platform upon which we may build a case for Christianity at work rests on six massive pillars: integrity, faithfulness, punctuality, quality workmanship, a pleasant attitude, and enthusiasm. Hire such a person and it will only be a matter of time before business will improve ... people will be impressed ... and Christianity will begin to seem important. — CHARLES R. SWINDOLL, *GROWING STRONG IN THE SEASONS OF LIFE*

ঞ্চ

Slaves, submit yourselves to your masters with all respect, not only to those who are good and considerate, but also to those who are harsh. For it is commendable if a man bears up under the pain of unjust suffering because he is conscious of God. — 1 PETER 2:18-19

ॐ

Masters, provide your slaves with what is right and fair, because you know that you also have a Master in heaven. — COLOSSIANS 4:1

ॐ

It is possible for business decisions to be made under a sense of the corporate leading of the Holy Spirit. . . . Business meetings should be viewed as worship services. Available facts can be presented and discussed, all with a view to listening to the voice of Christ. — RICHARD J. FOSTER, *CELEBRATION OF DISCIPLINE*

ॐ

Invest your work in the Savior's plan;
   Work hard for God and His will for man.
Don't count the hours that you toil and plod—
   You'll reap again all you do for God.
Don't waste your life for a passing joy;
   Don't sell your soul for a fragile toy!
Give till it hurts; give your very blood—
   You live but once; live all out for God.

          — WESLEY L. DUEWEL, *MEASURE YOUR LIFE*

⊄⅋

God asks us to lose so we can gain. He makes a hard request, then offers a promise. *Lose your selfish ambition; I will honor you for loving others. Lose your addiction to things; I will provide for you if you seek Me wholeheartedly. Lose your obsession to be in control; I will give you power as you follow Me.*
—BILL HYBELS, *DESCENDING INTO GREATNESS*

⊄⅋

As Christians, there is no shame in being obscure, if that is what God intends. Nor is there any honor in being famous, if we seek our own glory rather than God's. But there is shame and great loss when we refuse God's call, just as there is great honor when we seek to become all that he wants us to be in Christ. —JACK KUHATSCHEK, *THE SUPERMAN SYNDROME*

⊄⅋

Real integrity stays in place whether the test is adversity or prosperity. If you really have integrity, a demotion or promotion won't change you. Your inner care won't be dislodged. — CHARLES R. SWINDOLL, *THE BRIDE*

⊄⅋

Help me to see that I deny you in so many areas of my life, in so many ways and at so many different times. . . . When I steal something from another person to enrich or enhance my life—whether that be something material or some credit that is rightly due another, which I have claimed for myself—I deny you are the source of all blessings. —KEN GIRE, *INTIMATE MOMENTS WITH THE SAVIOR*

๛

The Bible repeatedly suggests a minimum giving standard of ten percent: the tithe. Giving the tithe allows us to express our thanksgiving for the privilege of earning wages, and also graphically demonstrates our understanding that we are not the owners of our resources; we are merely stewards of the money God has allowed us to earn. —BILL HYBELS, *HONEST TO GOD?*

๛

Woe to you Pharisees, because you give God a tenth of your mint, rue and all other kinds of garden herbs, but you neglect justice and the love of God. You should have practiced the latter without leaving the former undone. —LUKE 11:42

๛

Adversity or prosperity, both are tough tests on our balance. To stay balanced through adversity, resiliency is required. But to stay balanced through prosperity—ah, that demands *integrity*. The swift wind of compromise is a lot more devastating than the sudden jolt of misfortune. —CHARLES R. SWINDOLL, *GROWING STRONG IN THE SEASONS OF LIFE*

∂♪

Be careful about changing your standard so that it corresponds with your desires. Be very cautious about becoming inflated with thoughts of your own importance. Be alert to the pitfalls of prosperity and success. Should God grant riches, fame, and success, don't run scared or feel guilty. Just stay balanced. — CHARLES R. SWINDOLL, *GROWING STRONG IN THE SEASONS OF LIFE*

∂♪

Give attention to such characters as Nehemiah or Job (when he was healthy) or David or Paul. Mark these names down on the ledger of guys who recognized the value and joy of involvement and accomplishment outside the boundaries of their "stated" occupations. — CHARLES R. SWINDOLL, *GROWING STRONG IN THE SEASONS OF LIFE*

∂♪

God is in charge of my day . . . not I. While He is pleased with the wise management of time and intelligent planning from day to day, He is mainly concerned with the development of inner character. — CHARLES R. SWINDOLL, *GROWING STRONG IN THE SEASONS OF LIFE*

∂♪

I've been "one of the boys" throughout most of my professional career, yet I've never had to drink, gamble, or carouse with them. You don't have to do those things to get ahead. . . . Stay clean. Stay sober. Be a beacon to those around you who are in the dark. — BOB BRINER, *SQUEEZE PLAY*

♪

The accountability, love, and companionship of family and friends you can count on under normal circumstances is something you don't have when you're on the road. . . . Whenever possible, take a family member along with you on your business trips. . . . As your salary increases and your kids get older, . . . take your wife along as often as possible. . . . When your children are old enough, be sure to take each one separately on as many of your business trips as possible. . . . By all means, use the time alone in your hotel room to get caught up on your Bible reading and prayer. — BOB BRINER, *SQUEEZE PLAY*

♪

Seeking a promotion or working on climbing the ladder to success? Why not let God decide when and how you should be exalted. *Quietly* trust Him with your job or career. — CHARLES R. SWINDOLL, *GROWING STRONG IN THE SEASONS OF LIFE*

♪

Want your associates at work to be cheery, unselfish, free from catty, caustic comments and ugly glares? The place to begin is with that person who glares back at you from the bathroom mirror every morning. —CHARLES R. SWINDOLL, *GROWING STRONG IN THE SEASONS OF LIFE*

It's a wonder to me that practical business people avoid looking in the direction of inner or spiritual guidance for solving their problems. . . . Somehow, organized religion has not connected the idea of God with the nitty-gritty problems people face every day. If faith in God does not help people solve baffling personnel problems that come up in their organizations, or if it serves no purpose in working through the painful issues of downsizing or cutting costs or reengineering, then what good is it?
—DON SHULA & KEN BLANCHARD, *EVERYONE'S A COACH*

If finding God's way in the suddenness of storms makes our faith grow broad, then trusting God's wisdom in the "dailyness" of living makes it grow deep. And strong. —CHARLES R. SWINDOLL, *GROWING STRONG IN THE SEASONS OF LIFE*

Wisdom For . . . Being A Spiritual Leader

Remember your leaders, who spoke the word of God to you. Consider the outcome of their way of life and imitate their faith. —HEBREWS 13:7

※

There is no higher calling than to represent God to someone by living the life of a spiritual father before them. —DR. LARRY CRABB, *THE SILENCE OF ADAM*

※

Instruct a wise man and he will be wiser still; teach a righteous man and he will add to his learning. The fear of the LORD is the beginning of wisdom, and knowledge of the Holy One is understanding. —PROVERBS 9:9–10

※

You can always benefit from the help of someone else—to hone, to sharpen you. Leadership requires accountability. You never get too old to be taught a new truth. Discernment says, "I know that my knowledge is limited. Others can help me. I am open and ready to learn." — CHARLES R. SWINDOLL, *GROWING DEEP*

❧

Obey your leaders and submit to their authority. They keep watch over you as men who must give an account. Obey them so that their work will be a joy, not a burden, for that would be of no advantage to you. — HEBREWS 13:17

❧

For the LORD gives wisdom, and from his mouth come knowledge and understanding. — PROVERBS 2:6

❧

Spiritual leaders . . . are not made by majority vote or ecclesiastical decisions, by conferences or synods. Only God can make them! — CHARLES R. SWINDOLL, *GROWING STRONG IN THE SEASONS OF LIFE*

❧

A leader, obviously, must have some God-given natural qualities that cause others to respond to his . . . *influence*. At the same time, the *Christian* leader must possess a marked degree of Spirit-directed, humble devotion to the Lord Jesus Christ . . . lest he fall into the category of a self-appointed, ambitious creature who simply loves the spotlight. — CHARLES R. SWINDOLL, *GROWING STRONG IN THE SEASONS OF LIFE*

ఎ

Sitting down, Jesus called the Twelve and said, "If anyone wants to be first, he must be the very last, and the servant of all." —MARK 9:35

ఎ

Manly men release others from their control and encourage them with their influence. They touch their wives, children, and friends in sensitive ways that free them to struggle with *their* loneliness and selfishness and pain. Manly men nudge their family and friends to the same crossroads where they, as men, have found that trust or unbelief must be chosen. —DR. LARRY CRABB, *THE SILENCE OF ADAM*

ఎ

It is not true that husbands possess authority and wives have none. Each has been granted equal authority under God to serve the other. Authority is fundamentally authority to serve, not to lead. —DR. LARRY CRABB, *MEN & WOMEN: ENJOYING THE DIFFERENCE*

ఎ

The authority of a husband to serve his wife is distinct from the authority of a wife to serve her husband. The distinction in authority is not imposed by fiat, it rather grows out of distinctive resources for service in men and women. — DR. LARRY CRABB, *MEN & WOMEN: ENJOYING THE DIFFERENCE*

❧

We have different gifts, according to the grace given us. . . . If it is serving, let him serve; if it is teaching, let him teach; if it is encouraging, let him encourage; if it is contributing to the needs of others, let him give generously; if it is leadership, let him govern diligently. —ROMANS 12:6–8a

❧

Now the overseer must be above reproach, the husband of but one wife, temperate, self-controlled, respectable, hospitable, able to teach, not given to drunkenness, not violent but gentle, not quarrelsome, not a lover of money. He must manage his own family well and see that his children obey him with proper respect. —1 TIMOTHY 3:2–4

❧

It is refreshing when the dad is the one who sets the pace, who takes the lead, who, more than anyone in the family, "hungers and thirsts after righteousness" . . . where Christ is truly living out His life in the man of the house . . . where the wife and the children learn from the man's example what it means to truly love God. —CHARLES R. SWINDOLL, *THE STRONG FAMILY*

❧

Anyone who breaks one of the least of these commandments and teaches others to do the same will be called least in the kingdom of heaven, but whoever practices and teaches these commands will be called great in the kingdom of heaven. — MATTHEW 5:19

٭

Until I come, devote yourself to the public reading of Scripture, to preaching and to teaching. — 1 TIMOTHY 4:13

٭

The elders who direct the affairs of the church well are worthy of double honor, especially those whose work is preaching and teaching. — 1 TIMOTHY 5:17

٭

There is a transfer of wisdom from one life to another through the vehicle of the tongue.

What power! A fountain of life. An instrument of forgiveness. A concealment of violence. A source and/or transfer of wisdom. — CHARLES R. SWINDOLL, *GROWING DEEP*

٭

I have more insight than all my teachers, for I meditate on your statutes. I have more understanding than the elders, for I obey your precepts. — PSALM 119:99–100

٭

Do you want stability? Would you like insight? Is it your desire to have maturity? . . . All that—and so much more—can be found in God's reliable Word. . . . When it comes to a "final authority" in life, the Bible measures up. — CHARLES R. SWINDOLL, *GROWING DEEP*

∽

If I could have only one wish for God's people, it would be that all of us would return to the Word of God, that we would realize once for all that His Book has the answers. The Bible *is* the authority, the final resting place of our cares, our worries, our griefs, our tragedies, our sorrows, and our surprises. It is the final answer to our questions, our search. — CHARLES R. SWINDOLL, *GROWING DEEP*

∽

The fear of the LORD is the beginning of wisdom; all who follow his precepts have good understanding. To him belongs eternal praise. — PSALM 111:10

∽

The teaching of the wise is a fountain of life, turning a man from the snares of death. — PROVERBS 13:14

∽

Effective leaders have high integrity and are clear and straightforward in their interactions with others. — DON SHULA & KEN BLANCHARD, *EVERYONE'S A COACH*

❦

All Scripture is God-breathed and is useful for teaching, rebuking, correcting and training in righteousness, so that the man of God may be thoroughly equipped for every good work. —2 Timothy 3:16–17

❦

Speaking the truth in love, we will in all things grow up into him who is the Head, that is, Christ. From him the whole body, joined and held together by every supporting ligament, grows and builds itself up in love, as each part does its work. —Ephesians 4:15–16

❦

But the wisdom that comes from heaven is first of all pure; then peace-loving, considerate, submissive, full of mercy and good fruit, impartial and sincere. —James 3:17

❦

As long as you have credibility, you have leadership. To me, credibility is your people believing that what you say is something they can hang their hat on—something they can immediately believe and accept. —Don Shula & Ken Blanchard, *Everyone''s A Coach*

◇

Who is wise and understanding among you? Let him show it by his good life, by deeds done in the humility that comes from wisdom. — JAMES 3:13

◇

And the Lord's servant must not quarrel; instead, he must be kind to everyone, able to teach, not resentful. Those who oppose him he must gently instruct, in the hope that God will grant them repentance leading them to a knowledge of the truth. — 2 TIMOTHY 2:24–25

◇

The problem with most leaders today is they don't stand for anything. Leadership implies movement toward something, and convictions provide that direction. If you don't stand for something, you'll fall for anything. — DON SHULA & KEN BLANCHARD, EVERYONE'S A COACH

◇

The reason leaders today must begin with a strong vision, and a set of positive beliefs that support it, is that without them, the people they're coaching will not only lose, they'll be lost. Lacking something to uplift their hearts when difficulties arise, their minds will not be equal to the challenge. — DON SHULA & KEN BLANCHARD, EVERYONE'S A COACH

∂∕ℓ

Be shepherds of God's flock that is under your care, serving as overseers—not because you must, but because you are willing, as God wants you to be; not greedy for money, but eager to serve; not lording it over those entrusted to you, but being examples to the flock. — 1 PETER 5:2–3

∂∕ℓ

I challenge you each morning to get down on your knees and seek God's power to keep you a loving, humble, and effective leader (or parent)—for *His* glory, not yours. —CHARLES R. SWINDOLL, *GROWING STRONG IN THE SEASONS OF LIFE*

∂∕ℓ

Encourage and rebuke with all authority. Do not let anyone despise you. — TITUS 2:15b

∂∕ℓ

You must teach what is in accord with sound doctrine. Teach the older men to be temperate, worthy of respect, self-controlled, and sound in faith, in love and in endurance. — TITUS 2:1–2

∂∕ℓ

Encourage the young men to be self-controlled. In everything set them an example by doing what is good. In your teaching show integrity, seriousness and soundness of speech that cannot be condemned, so that those who oppose you may be ashamed because they have nothing bad to say about us. — Titus 2:6–8

༄

Be strong in the Lord and in his mighty power. Put on the full armor of God so that you can take your stand against the devil's schemes. For our struggle is not against flesh and blood, but against the rulers, against the authorities, against the powers of this dark world and against the spiritual forces of evil in the heavenly realms. — Ephesians 6:10–12

༄

Let us consider how we may spur one another on toward love and good deeds. . . . Let us encourage one another-and all the more as you see the Day approaching. — Hebrews 10:24–25

༄

People who serve for the right reason and in the right place are enthusiastic and effective. Their teaching has impact. Their hospitality is warm. Their counsel is wise. Their leadership is strong. Their administration is efficient. Their evangelism is fruitful. Their mercy is heartfelt. — Bill Hybels, *Honest To God?*

Wisdom For ... Being A Good Neighbor

You are the salt of the earth.... You are the light of the world. A city on a hill cannot be hidden. Neither do people light a lamp and put it under a bowl. Instead they put it on its stand, and it gives light to everyone in the house. In the same way, let your light shine before men, that they may see your good deeds and praise your Father in heaven. —MATTHEW 5:13–16

ൖ

"You are the salt of the earth," said Jesus. "You are the light on a hill. Don't put a bushel basket over it." Let the light shine. Let the salt bite. That's your role, Christian! The world expects it from us even though it doesn't agree. —CHARLES R. SWINDOLL, *GROWING DEEP*

ൖ

I urge you to tell others about the Gospel of Jesus Christ, and then about the values of the cultural mandate.

There is no way this country is going to be changed without a renewal of faith and a new commitment to our Savior. —D. JAMES KENNEDY, *CHARACTER & DESTINY*

ঔ৯

A new command I give you: Love one another. As I have loved you, so you must love one another. By this all men will know that you are my disciples, if you love one another. —JOHN 13:34–35

ঔ৯

Live as children of light (for the fruit of the light consists in all goodness, righteousness and truth) and find out what pleases the Lord. Have nothing to do with the fruitless deeds of darkness, but rather expose them. —EPHESIANS 5:8a–11

ঔ৯

Help me to realize that no matter how violent their opposition, people are not the enemy. They are prisoners of the enemy. Help me to realize that you died to free those prisoners. —KEN GIRE, *INTIMATE MOMENTS WITH THE SAVIOR*

ঔ৯

Do not resist an evil person. If someone strikes you on the right cheek, turn to him the other also. And if someone wants to sue you and take your tunic, let him have your cloak as well. If someone forces you to go one mile, go with him two miles. Give to the one who asks you, and do not turn away from the one who wants to borrow from you. — MATTHEW 5:39–42

✌

Do not withhold good from those who deserve it, when it is in your power to act. Do not say to your neighbor, "Come back later; I'll give it tomorrow"—when you now have it with you. — PROVERBS 3:27–28

✌

Give me a heart of compassion that I may love my neighbor the way the good Samaritan loved his. Give me eyes that do not look away and feet that do not turn to the other side of the road. — KEN GIRE, *INSTRUCTIVE MOMENTS WITH THE SAVIOR*

✌

Help me to realize that just as I brought nothing into this world, so I can take nothing out, and that the only riches I will have in heaven are those which have gone before me, the riches which I have placed in the hands of the poor for your safekeeping. — KEN GIRE, *INSTRUCTIVE MOMENTS WITH THE SAVIOR*

✌

Give to everyone who asks you, and if anyone takes what belongs to you, do not demand it back. Do to others as you would have them do to you. — LUKE 6:30–31

❧

If anyone has material possessions and sees his brother in need but has no pity on him, how can the love of God be in him? Dear children, let us not love with words or tongue but with actions and in truth. —1 JOHN 3:17–18

❧

He who despises his neighbor sins, but blessed is he who is kind to the needy. —PROVERBS 14:21

❧

Help me to realize that although I cannot do everything to alleviate the suffering in this world, I can do something. And even if that something is a very little thing, it is better than turning my head and walking away. —KEN GIRE, *INSTRUCTIVE MOMENTS WITH THE SAVIOR*

❧

Help me to see that . . . when I turn my head from the hungry and the homeless, I deny that you are a God of mercy who has put me here to be your hands and your feet. —KEN GIRE, *INTIMATE MOMENTS WITH THE SAVIOR*

❧

The one who sows to please the Spirit, from the Spirit will reap eternal life. Let us not become weary in doing good, for at the proper time we will reap a harvest if we do not give up. Therefore, as we have opportunity, let us do good to all people, especially to those who belong to the family of believers. — GALATIANS 6:8–10

ЫР

Do not judge, and you will not be judged. Do not condemn, and you will not be condemned. Forgive, and you will be forgiven. Give, and it will be given to you. A good measure, pressed down, shaken together and running over, will be poured into your lap. For with the measure you use, it will be measured to you. — LUKE 6:37–38

ЫР

Live in harmony with one another. Do not be proud, but be willing to associate with people of low position. Do not be conceited. — ROMANS 12:16

ЫР

In demonstrating what it meant to be a good neighbor, the Samaritan defined the meaning of love. Love doesn't look away. And it doesn't walk away. It involves itself. It inconveniences itself. It indebts itself. — KEN GIRE, *INSTRUCTIVE MOMENTS WITH THE SAVIOR*

ЫР

Modern progress has made the world a neighbourhood: God has given us the task of making it a brotherhood. — PHILIP GIBBS, *YOU CAN SAY THAT AGAIN* (COMPILED AND ARRANGED BY R. E. O. WHITE)

❧

The important thing from God's perspective is not merely hiding the truth in our hearts but sharing it with the world around us. It is not enough to hide our light under a bushel, as the verse says, but to reveal the light of truth to a world dying in sin. When it comes to sharing our faith and impacting our culture, silence is far from golden. —D. JAMES KENNEDY, *CHARACTER & DESTINY*

❧

Be very careful, then, how you live—not as unwise but as wise, making the most of every opportunity, because the days are evil. —EPHESIANS 5:15–16

❧

LORD, who may dwell in your sanctuary? Who may live on your holy hill? He whose walk is blameless and who does what is righteous, who speaks the truth from his heart and has no slander on his tongue, who does his neighbor no wrong and casts no slur on his fellowman. —PSALMS 15:1–3

❧

We who are strong ought to bear with the failings of the weak and not to please ourselves. Each of us should please his neighbor for his good, to build him up. —ROMANS 15:1–2

❧

Forgive me, Lord, for being so concerned about my other commitments that I am unconcerned about my commitment to others. Help me to realize that so much of true ministry is not what I schedule but what comes as an intrusion to my schedule. —KEN GIRE, *INSTRUCTIVE MOMENTS WITH THE SAVIOR*

❧

Love does no harm to its neighbor. Therefore love is the fulfillment of the law. —ROMANS 13:10

❧

Do not plot harm against your neighbor, who lives trustfully near you. Do not accuse a man for no reason— when he has done you no harm. —PROVERBS 3:29–30

❧

Do not hate your brother in your heart. Rebuke your neighbor frankly so you will not share in his guilt. Do not seek revenge or bear a grudge against one of your people, but love your neighbor as yourself. —LEVITICUS 19:17–18a

❧

There is an idea abroad among moral people that they should make their neighbours good. One person I have to make good—myself. My duty to my neighbour is much more nearly expressed by saying that I have to make him happy, if I may. —Robert Louis Stevenson, *You Can Say That Again* (compiled and arranged by R. E. O. White)

҈

Get rid of all bitterness, rage and anger, brawling and slander, along with every form of malice. Be kind and compassionate to one another, forgiving each other, just as in Christ God forgave you. —Ephesians 4:31–32

҈

Therefore each of you must put off falsehood and speak truthfully to his neighbor, for we are all members of one body. —Ephesians 4:25

҈

You shall not give false testimony against your neighbor. You shall not covet your neighbor's house. You shall not covet your neighbor's wife, or his manservant or maidservant, his ox or donkey, or anything that belongs to your neighbor. —Exodus 20:16–17

҈

O Lord, help me to love my enemies and to pray for those who persecute me or who, in some way, betray me. Help me not to trade insult for insult or injury for injury. Help me to give a blessing instead. —Ken Gire, *Intimate Moments With The Savior*

◌◌

Seldom set foot in your neighbor's house—too much of you, and he will hate you. —Proverbs 25:17

◌◌

A man who lacks judgment derides his neighbor, but a man of understanding holds his tongue. — Proverbs 11:12

◌◌

Do not testify against your neighbor without cause, or use your lips to deceive. Do not say, "I'll do to him as he has done to me; I'll pay that man back for what he did." —Proverbs 24:28–29

◌◌

When asked about the two greatest commands, Jesus replied: to love God and to love others. That is what motivated Jesus, and that is what is to motivate us. —Bill Hybels, *Descending Into Greatness*

ACKNOWLEDGMENTS

Mel Blount: THE CROSS BURNS BRIGHTLY by Mel Blount with Cynthia Sterling. Copyright© 1993 by Mel Blount. Used by permission of Zondervan Publishing House.

Bob Briner: SQUEEZE PLAY by Bob Briner. Copyright© 1994 by Bob Briner. Used by permission of Zondervan Publishing House.

Dennis Byrd: RISE AND WALK by Dennis Byrd with Michael D'Orso. Copyright© 1993 by Dennis Byrd and Michael D'Orso. Used by permission of Zondervan Publishing House.

Lawrence J. Crabb: THE SILENCE OF ADAM by Larry Crabb with Don Hudson and Al Andrews. Copyright© 1995 by Larry Crabb. Used by permission of Zondervan Publishing House.

Lawrence J. Crabb: MEN & WOMEN: ENJOYING THE DIFFERENCE by Larry Crabb. Copyright© 1991 by Larry Crabb. Used by permission of Zondervan Publishing House.

Ken Davis: FIRE UP YOUR LIFE! by Ken Davis. Copyright© 1995 by Ken Davis. Used by permission of Zondervan Publishing House.

Dave Dravecky: WHEN YOU CAN'T COME BACK by Dave and Jan Dravecky with Ken Gire. Copyright© 1992 by Dave Dravecky. Used by permission of Zondervan Publishing House.

Wesley L. Duewel: MEASURE YOUR LIFE by Wesley L. Duewel. Copyright© 1992 by Wesley L. Duewel. Used by permission of Zondervan Publishing House.

Richard J. Foster: CELEBRATION OF DISCIPLINE by Richard J. Foster. Copyright© 1978 by Richard J. Foster. Used by permission of Zondervan Publishing House.

Ken Gire: INCREDIBLE MOMENTS WITH THE SAVIOR by Ken Gire. Copyright© 1990 by Ken Gire. Used by permission of Zondervan Publishing House.

Ken Gire: INSTRUCTIVE MOMENTS WITH THE SAVIOR by Ken Gire. Copyright© 1992 by Ken Gire. Used by permission of Zondervan Publishing House.

Ken Gire: INTIMATE MOMENTS WITH THE SAVIOR by Ken Gire. Copyright© 1989 by Ken Gire. Used by permission of Zondervan Publishing House.

Bill Hybels: DESCENDING INTO GREATNESS by Bill Hybels and Rob Wilkins. Copyright© 1993 by Bill Hybels. Used by permission of Zondervan Publishing House.

Bill Hybels: HONEST TO GOD? by Bill Hybels. Copyright© 1990 by Bill Hybels. Used by permission of Zondervan Publishing House.

D. James Kennedy: CHARACTER & DESTINY by D. James Kennedy with James Nelson Black. Copyright© 1994 by D. James Kennedy. Used by permission of Zondervan Publishing House.

Jack Kuhatschek: THE SUPERMAN SYNDROME by Jack Kuhatschek. Copyright© 1995 by Jack Kuhatschek. Used by permission of Zondervan Publishing House.